THE POETRY OF LIVERMORIUM

The Poetry of Livermorium

Walter the Educator

Silent King Books

SILENT KING BOOKS

SKB

Copyright © 2024 by Walter the Educator

All rights reserved. No part of this book may be reproduced in any manner whatsoever without written permission except in the case of brief quotations embodied in critical articles and reviews.

First Printing, 2024

Disclaimer
This book is a literary work; poems are not about specific persons, locations, situations, and/or circumstances unless mentioned in a historical context. This book is for entertainment and informational purposes only. The author and publisher offer this information without warranties expressed or implied. No matter the grounds, neither the author nor the publisher will be accountable for any losses, injuries, or other damages caused by the reader's use of this book. The use of this book acknowledges an understanding and acceptance of this disclaimer.

"Earning a degree in chemistry changed my life!"
- Walter the Educator

dedicated to all the chemistry lovers, like myself, across the world

LIVERMORIUM

In a world of elements, obscure yet bright,

LIVERMORIUM

There dwells Livermorium, a wondrous light.

LIVERMORIUM

Born from the fusion of atoms' dance,

LIVERMORIUM

In laboratories, where scientists prance.

LIVERMORIUM

Named after Livermore, a place of science's quest,

LIVERMORIUM

In its nucleus, secrets divest.

LIVERMORIUM

Protons and neutrons, tightly packed,

LIVERMORIUM

In quantum realms, where mysteries are stacked.

LIVERMORIUM

A fleeting existence, it swiftly decays,

LIVERMORIUM

A transient beauty in ephemeral displays.

LIVERMORIUM

But in its essence, a story unfolds,

LIVERMORIUM

Of particles bound in quantum molds.

LIVERMORIUM

A fusion of californium and calcium's dance,

LIVERMORIUM

Creates Livermorium in a fleeting trance.

LIVERMORIUM

Its atomic number, one one six,

LIVERMORIUM

In periodic tales, where elements mix.

LIVERMORIUM

In the heart of a reactor, where particles collide,

LIVERMORIUM

Livermorium emerges, a fleeting stride.

LIVERMORIUM

Unstable and swift, it yearns to be free,

LIVERMORIUM

A testament to nature's grand decree.

LIVERMORIUM

In laboratories of innovation's might,

LIVERMORIUM

Scientists harness its transient light.

LIVERMORIUM

Unveiling the secrets of atomic dance,

LIVERMORIUM

In the pursuit of knowledge's advance.

LIVERMORIUM

Oh Livermorium, elusive and rare,

LIVERMORIUM

In the cosmos' tapestry, you boldly dare.

LIVERMORIUM

To challenge the laws of space and time,

LIVERMORIUM

In the quest for understanding sublime.

LIVERMORIUM

Your electrons whirl in quantum ballet,

LIVERMORIUM

A symphony of motion in cosmic array.

LIVERMORIUM

Bound by forces, both strong and weak,

LIVERMORIUM

In the fabric of reality, you speak.

LIVERMORIUM

From the depths of the atom's core,

LIVERMORIUM

To the farthest reaches of cosmic lore,

LIVERMORIUM

Livermorium whispers secrets profound,

LIVERMORIUM

In the silent language of particles unbound.

LIVERMORIUM

In the crucible of creation, where stars are born,

LIVERMORIUM

Livermorium dances, a cosmic thorn.

LIVERMORIUM

A fleeting glimpse of the universe's plan,

LIVERMORIUM

In the grand tapestry of existence, where all began.

LIVERMORIUM

So let us marvel at Livermorium's flight,

LIVERMORIUM

A beacon of knowledge in the endless night.

LIVERMORIUM

For in its fleeting existence, we find,

LIVERMORIUM

The essence of creation, both wondrous and kind.

LIVERMORIUM

ABOUT THE CREATOR

Walter the Educator is one of the pseudonyms for Walter Anderson. Formally educated in Chemistry, Business, and Education, he is an educator, an author, a diverse entrepreneur, and he is the son of a disabled war veteran. "Walter the Educator" shares his time between educating and creating. He holds interests and owns several creative projects that entertain, enlighten, enhance, and educate, hoping to inspire and motivate you.

Follow, find new works, and stay up to date
with Walter the Educator™
at WaltertheEducator.com

www.ingramcontent.com/pod-product-compliance
Lightning Source LLC
LaVergne TN
LVHW020134080526
838201LV00119B/3866